haiku & zen

I0231313

Poems and Images by:
Orlino C. Baldonado

Digital Artwork and Layout by:
Rosanna R. Dalilis & Melvin S. Dato

Published by:

ec&media
STORIES • VIDEOS • MUSIC

10511 Hardin Valley Road, Knoxville, Tennessee USA 37932
Contact: orlinob@gmail.com

ISBN: 978-1-948623-68-1

General Table of Contents

Haiku and Zen

Introduction

This book merges two of my main interests: short poems (as reader and writer) and minimalist art (especially Zen photos and artwork).

In 2009, I compiled many of the haiku poems I wrote over the years. I was encouraged to write them after a cursory look at the body of literature available then, which expanded my concept of what haikus are. Then, my knowledge about haiku consisted of (1) Subject matter is about simple nature scenes and the feeling you get by observing these simple scenes, and (2) the strict 5-7-5 syllable count in three lines as the format for haiku poems. I also read some of the haiku poems written by my grandchildren and learned from them. Then, I read the latest Haiku Anthology, and I came to some conclusions regarding subject matter and format.

Subject Matter

Several haiku masters have greatly expanded the subject matters addressed in haikus, way beyond that of nature and the seasons. Some poets have included subjects like love, sorrow, death, disasters, people at work, etc.

I also expanded the scope of my haiku subjects beyond the nature-related themes.

I began thinking of haiku as describing images and photos – this is what we do mainly when we look at them on our phone, tablet, and computer screens. Thus, the use of haiku as a label evolved. This resulted in some of the haikus becoming labels for photos and images.

To stay within the spirit of other haiku poets who wrote thousands of haikus of haikus during the past five centuries, I added the emotion that specific images would evoke. This resulted in some of the haikus becoming labels for photos or images.

Number of Syllables and Format

In addition to expanding the subject matters, I investigated the constraints of the 5-7-5 or seventeen syllable format. This was necessary to properly address a given subject matter using several syllables.

The word "frog" is very short and only has one syllable, and so is "love," so when they are used in a haiku, these words take up only one syllable. To have a word like "insecurity" which has five syllables when used in a haiku will take up five syllables of the seventeen syllables in a 5-7-5 format. Not much is left for the other words. Thus, the use of the 5-7-5 format would be too constraining.

I began to experiment with the 6-9-6 and the 5-9-7 formats and the two-line format instead of the traditional three lines. The poems with these extended formats still read and felt satisfactory. Also, I began to see haikus in one-line and single-line formats in the magazines.

And thus, with the relaxation of the traditions and usual practices, I was able to address other subjects.

Titles for Haikus

Haikus are very short and often have no title. How would we conveniently refer to a specific haiku if there is no title? Take for example Basho's Furuike or pond and frog haiku:

> *Furuike ya*
> *Kawasu tobikumu*
> *Mizo no ato.*

Which translates to:
> The old pond
> A frog jumps in
> Sound of water.

There is no title, and if the master had written other haikus involving ponds and frogs, we would be forced to distinguish this from others.

The Haiku Anthology has arranged the haikus by the poets' name but no titles. It would have been easier to refer to a specific haiku if there was a title. In discussing Basho's frog haiku, since it does not have a title, it would be easier to refer to it by title if it had one, and not just by subject matter.

It is a matter of convenience. In this book, I have added a title to each haiku.

Haiku in this Book

The collection of two hundred eight (278) haikus in this book came from a set of over 500 that I wrote through the years. I have assigned a title to each one.

I still had to impose discipline. I still prefer the traditional 5-7-5 syllables in a three-line format. I kept the number of syllables in one line to a minimum, even if a haiku did not strictly follow the 5-7-5 syllable format.

Haiku Subject Matters

I established eight general subject matters for my haikus in this book. These categories are:

1. Seasons and Weather
2. Busy People
3. Man-made Places
4. Flora (Plants)
5. Fauna (Creatures and Animals)
6. Earth Features
7. Sky and Moon
8. Feelings and Reflections

Several haikus were written for each category. More accurately, I sorted the haikus I had written, and the categories appeared. The split was not always clear, but it provided a way to sort the 278 haikus included in this book.

On the Zen Images

The Zen images (one per set of three haikus) are not in any specific order. A title was assigned to each image and entered alphabetically, for convenience.

Most of the images came from photos I had taken (using film). They were slightly edited to fit a "minimalist style" in the tradition of thinking haiku as a minimalist style of poetry. Most of these images were in color and I simplified them by removing color. Viewing these images in black and white, and comparing them to the original colored images did not seem to dilute their beauty; in fact, the monochrome gray color adds to the enjoyment of the patterns and images.

The images are to be viewed independently of the haiku poems; there was no attempt to attach an image to a specific haiku.

What Good are These?

Haikus provide a simplified way of looking at and reacting to our increasingly complex world.

I hope the reader will enjoy a few of the haikus here. If so, then my time and the efforts of the people who helped me in producing this book would have been worth it.

I hope that this adds to the pile of books on the subject and contributes something to the ever-growing field of literature for the fans of haiku and Zen images.

Orlino C, Baldonado, PhD

10511 Hardin Valley Road, Knoxville, Tennessee USA 37932
ecEmedia Inc., Publisher
Contact: orlinob@gmail.com

Section 1
Weather and Seasons

1-00 Seasons

Change, change, change, and change.
Each time, a renewed feeling
To adjust and enjoy.

TABLE OF CONTENTS - SECTION 1

TITLE   **PAGE**

1-01 Autumn

Fall season means crisp air
Leaf colors turn to gold and red.
Prepare for Winter.

1-02 Autumn Foliage Change

Green foliage turns gold
Makes the landscape colorful.
The season is changing.

1-03 Buds in Spring

Pink clustered blossoms
Cling to branches of bare trees.
Spring has arrived.

Z1-1 Spring-Branch

1-04   Dark Nights

Deep sighs, far away gazing,
Searching the voids of dark nights
Cicadas crack the gloom.

1-05   Drought

Parched land, wilting plants
Waiting, hoping for moisture
All adjust and endure.

1-06   Dry Season

Rains are rare, plants wilt
Grass turns brown, roads get dusty
Water is scarce.

Z1-2 Wall-Plants-Diamond

1-07   Evening

Sultry air, sticky sweat
Harried bees busy with the late bloom.
Fireflies prepare to shine.

1-08   Fall leaves

A walk in the woods,
Feel leaves crunch under my feet.
I take in the crisp air.

1-09   Fog

Early morning fog
Cloaks the landscape with white mist.
It is quiet; there is no color.

Z1-3 Flowers-and-Stems3

1-10   Harvest Time

All the hard work is done.
It's time to gather the earth's bounty
And pause in gratitude.

1-11   Lazy Afternoon

Empty park benches,
Humid air hangs thick and low.
It's a lazy afternoon.

1-12   Maple Leaves

Reddish maple leaves
Among the yellow-green leaves
Speak of autumn's arrival.

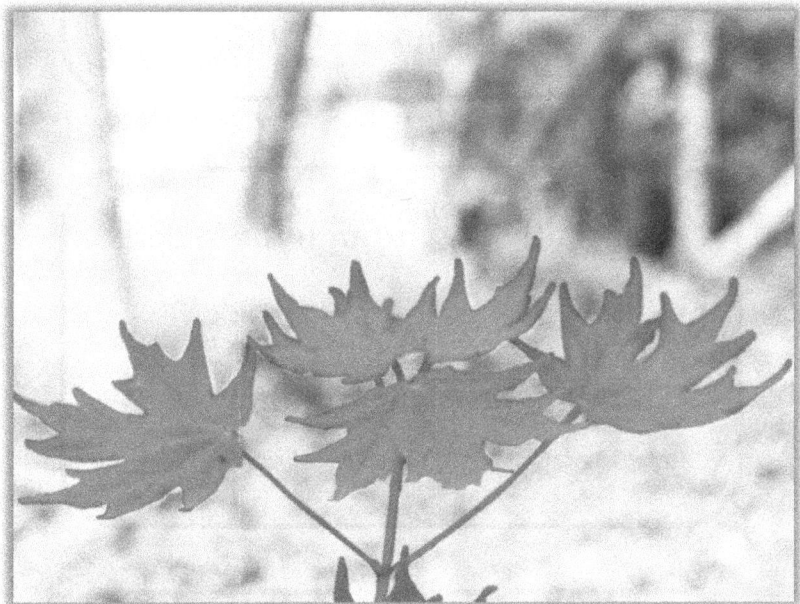

Z1-4 Maple-Leaves

1-13 Mist

Mist floats over the lake
Warmed by the early summer sun,
A clear sign of autumn.

1-14 Pathway through the Woods

Path strewn with leaves
Through the silent autumn woods.
Feeling nature's best.

1-15 Planting Time

Early spring soil gets warm.
Sow seeds, they germinate, then grow.
Witness life renewed.

Z1-5 Lights-and-Clouds

1-16 Rain and Sunshine

Rain and sunshine
One defines the other.
We need them both.

1-17 Raindrops on Pavement

Drops on hard pavement
Later join, causing a deluge.
Rain clouds cover the sun.

1-18 Rainstorm

The sky rumbles
Lightning flashes bright with zit zat.
There's a summer rainstorm.

Z1-6 Beach-Scene-Florida

1-19 Rice Planting

Rains soaked the dry soil.
Plowed, harrowed, it becomes a slurry.
Time to plant the rice seedlings.

1-20 Shrouds of Mist

Shrouds of mist draped over
Verdant slopes and highways.
Drive through the silent fog.

1-21 Snowfall

Soft silent snowfalls
Blanket the dreary landscape.
Dark bare trees on white.

Z1-7 Snow-on-Ground-with-Trees

1-22 Spring

Spring awakens life.
Flowers bloom, birds chirp, and bees buzz.
Life renews once more.

1-23 Stark Winter Branches

Leaves are gone, branches bare,
Gray against the blue sky,
Waiting return of green foliage.

1-24 Summer

Summers are hot and warm
Hurriedly work, the rest.
Sadly, it ends too soon.

Z1-8 Snow-on-Branches

1-25 Walk Through Woods

A brisk walk through the woods
Cleanses the mind and body.
Nature's healing embrace.

1-26 Wind blowing

Wind blowing southwest
Fallen dried leaves flow past me.
Clouds soon turn to rain.

1-27 Winter

Winter is cold and dreary.
Snow, ice, cold rains, bare trees,
Reflect and think by the fireplace.

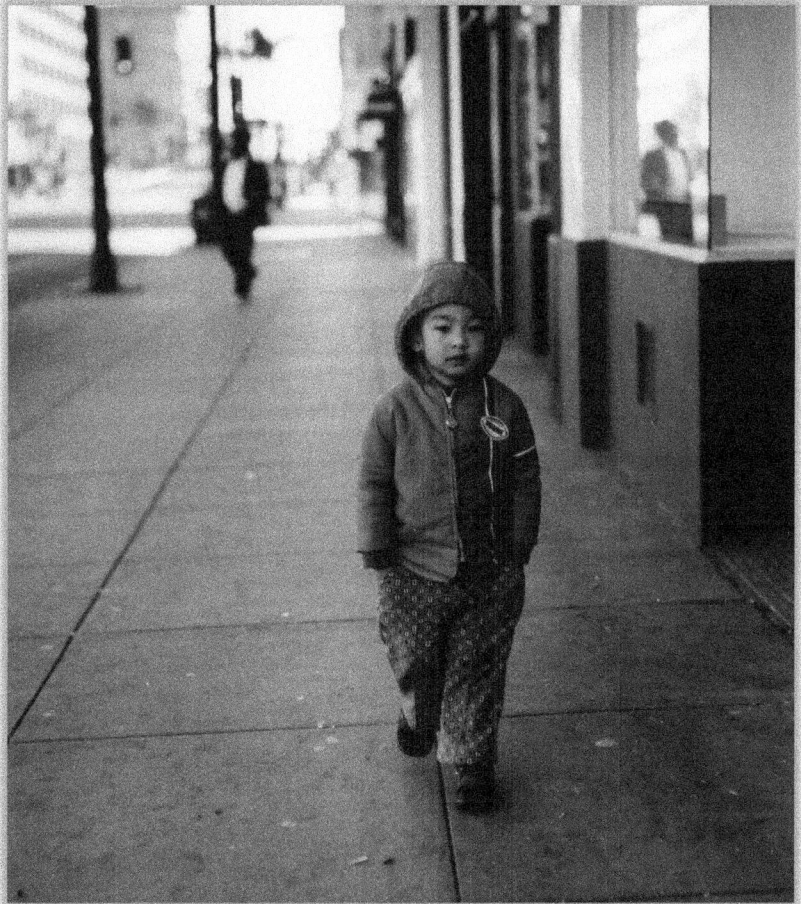

Z1-9 Boy-Walking

Section 2
Busy People

2-00 Human Beings

Humans populate,
Disperse over the entire planet.
They dominate all.

TABLE OF CONTENTS- SECTION 2

2-01 Aircraft Carrier Launches

Jet engines whining
Catapults help propel the fighter jet.
Feel sheer terror and excitement.

2-02 Ball Game

Bleachers full, hearts beat.
The ball quickly moves between players.
Game shows youth at play.

2-03 Carabao Pulling Plow

Strong carabao
Pulls plow to till the land,
A farmer's partner.

Z2-1 Carabao-and-Farmer

2-04 Cell Phone Use

The cell phone is always on
People stare at it constantly.
Pacifier for all.

2-05 Children

Children let us go on,
Provide a link to forever.
They are the future.

2-06 Church & Religion

The faithful gather.
They bow, pray, sing, and ask for mercy
To a God who might not answer.

Z2-2 Girl-and-Pier

2-07 Construction Work

Despite grime and heat
Men and machine move materials
To build a structure.

2-08 Corn Combines

Combines cut cornrows
Separate the seeds from the chaff,
Gather yellow gold.

2-09 Fans for Baby

She is new but has already
Conquered all around her.
They become lifelong fans.

Z2-3 Construction-Unloading

2-10 Farm Work

The land gives bounty.
It must be worked on
Or else it gets fallow.

2-11 Flower Floats

Flowers cover large floats,
Like insects crawling to display
Their grandeur for many eyes.

2-12 Elephant at Work

Majestic animal at work
Move objects with its trunk.
It's an organic machine.

Z2-4 Playing-Under-Elephant-Sculpture

2-13 Entering College

High school friendships end.
New classmates become friends.
A new life starts.

2-14 First Day in School

First day in school.
Parting fear turns to excitement.
Tomorrow is better.

2-15 Flag

Stars and stripes
In flag, waving proud and high.
Symbol of a nation.

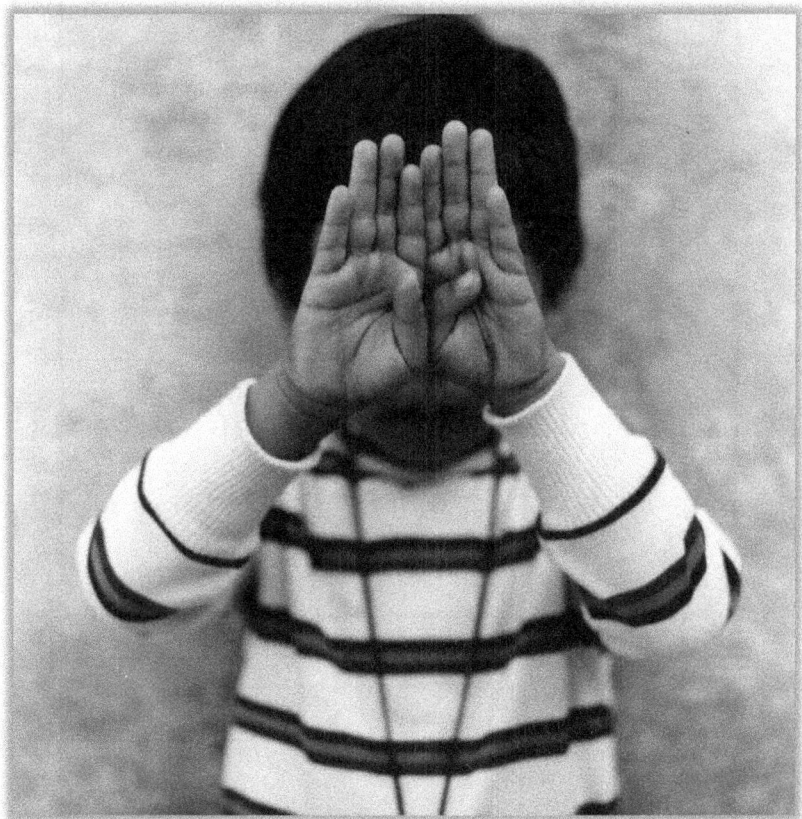

Z2-5 Boy-and-Hands

2-16 Grandkids

Grandkids are links to forever
Their parents are the present
And grandkids are the future.

2-17 Health

Feelings of good health
As if we can go on and on.
We enjoy living.

2-18 Highway

Highway lights passed by
As the cars covered the miles.
All anxious for home.

Z2-6 Girl-and-Water-Fountain

2-19 Horse Racing

Muscles purr, hooves race.
Horses urged to be in front.
Hopeful people are yelling.

2-20 Life's Beginning

Life evolves and goes on
To produce and reproduce.
It will last briefly.

2-21 Life's Ending

Daily, we strive to survive
For our lives to continue,
But grateful they end.

Z2-7 Honeysuckle-Flower-Detail

2-22 Live Life Simply

Life is brief, fleeting,
Weighed down by useless burdens.
Just live life simply.

2-23 Machines and Things

Parts and pieces held
Together to work and run,
So we don't have to.

2-24 Making a Difference

We travel together.
Help others lighten their load.
This lightens our own.

Z2-8 Boy-and-Tree

2-25 Military Parade

All are in crisp uniforms.
Groups move in precise formations.
Drums enhance commands.

2-26 Office Work

Computer screens glare.
People stare at them all day,
Part of office work.

2-27 Parade

Drums loudly vibrate.
Band groups move in rhythm.
People line sidewalks.

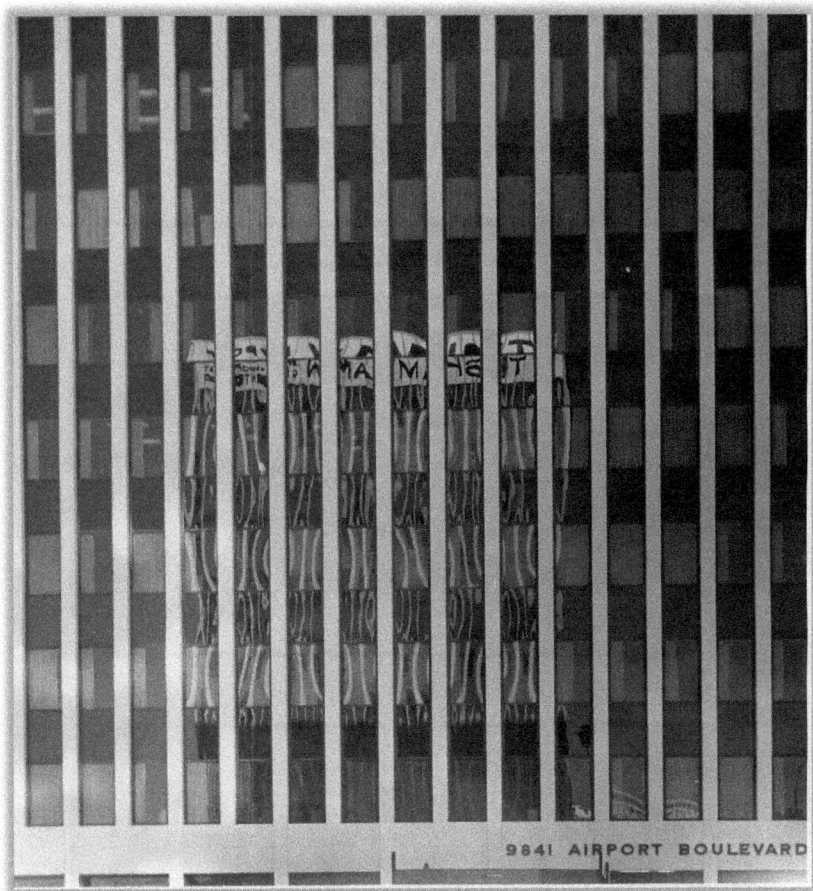

Z2-9 Building-Reflection

2-28 Politics

Silly serious acts
By tricky folks who promise much,
But don't deliver.

2-29 Singing

Singing frees the soul
And unburdens the heart.
Melodies endure.

2-30 Six o'clock Oration Bell

Church bells toll at six
Call for villagers to pray.
It marks the end of day.

Z2-10 Lake-Reflection

2-31   Slot Machines

Bets are made, symbols roll
Shiny slot machines tease,
Hearts flutter with each push.

2-32   Surgery

Lights on, blue hands hover
Patient unaware and under.
Part of the process to get well.

2-33   Tombstones

Still tombstones
Randomly placed or aligned
Mark our final place.

Z2-11 Graffiti

2-34 Truck Driving

Rumble increases, then wh-oo-z.
Eighteen-wheeler passes by,
Then the rumble recedes.

2-35 Village Morning

Wisps of smoke arise
From homes in villages,
Start the day for peasants.

2-36 Wheat Combines

Combines with giant arms
Harvest wheat in neat rows.
Machines scrape wide spaces.

Z2-12 Fishermen-Pulling-Net

Section 3
Man-made Places

3-00 Man-made Places

Creation of men,
Timeless places we visit,
Explore and admire.

TABLE OF CONTENTS– SECTION 3

TITLE   PAGE

3-01 Angkor Wat

Old Buddhist temples
Abandoned due to drought and deluge.
Plant roots took over.

3-02 Big Dam

Water flows into channels
To turn turbines and generators
To produce power for all.

3-03 Busy Airport

Check in security gates,
Have coffee, wait, and listen.
Eyes glued to screens.

Z3-1 Bamboo-Grove

3-04   Car Assembly Factory

Robots and people at work
In a choreographed factory
Make a car each minute.

3-05   Casino

Machines flash and entice.
You bet, watch shows, and eat.
Win or lose, you enjoy.

3-06   Cruise Ship

Cabins, safety rules
Food, drinks, song, dance, and sight-see,
All exhausted but happy.

Z3-2 Pottery-Market

3-07   Flowers in Fields

Flowers cover the land.
Colors and beauty are painted
Over the landscape.

3-08   Golf Course

Golf green and fairways,
Balls zip and roll to the hole.
Enjoy the trees and greens.

3-09   Grand Prix Race

Special racetrack
With Grand Prix cars racing,
Engines are whining hard.

Z3-3 Leaf-Patterns

3-10   Grocery Store

Shelves have everything
To buy and fill up carts.
Shoppers check their lists.

3-11   Home Garden

Small garden plot,
With lush plants tended daily,
A refuge from stress.

3-12   IMAX Theater

A giant screen surrounds you.
You can tour vast plains and deserts
Sitting inside in comfort.

Z3-4 Flowers-and-Stems1

3-13   Laboratory

People in lab coats and masks,
Glass tubes gurgle and percolate.
They write the results.

3-14   Las Vegas Strip

People gamble and watch shows,
Enjoy neon lights and displays,
Winning lights enthrall.

3-15   Los Angeles Freeway

Cars zip through freeways,
Follow signs and speed limits.
There is order in the chaos.

Z3-5 Lights-Atop-Pole2

3-16   Logical Way of Doing Things

Complex seems unknown.
Change complex to simple,
Simple becomes known.

3-17   McDonald's Fast Food

Big yellow arch sign
Appears above the night lights.
Customers need fast food.

3-18   Mississippi River

The river is huge
It is wide, murky, and silent.
It slices the land.

Z3-6 Metal-Plows-for Sale

3-19   Museums

Museums have artworks
Showing different artists,
Curated then admired.

3-20   Neat Lawns

Recently mowed lawns
Neatly trimmed hedges, clean paths
A day's work well done.

3-21   Niagara Falls

Flowing waters roar.
Niagara Falls flows incessantly.
Spray mists add to the menace.

Z3-7 Sculpture-Relief

3-22 NY Oculus

Modern huge white cave
Immortalizes tragic 911 events,
Displays man's creative talent.

3-23 Oak Alley Plantation

Twenty-eight large oaks
Lead to the old plantation house
Awesome in size and age.

3-24 Play Stadium

Fans in hats and shirts
Watch the game at the stadium,
Get excited in unison.

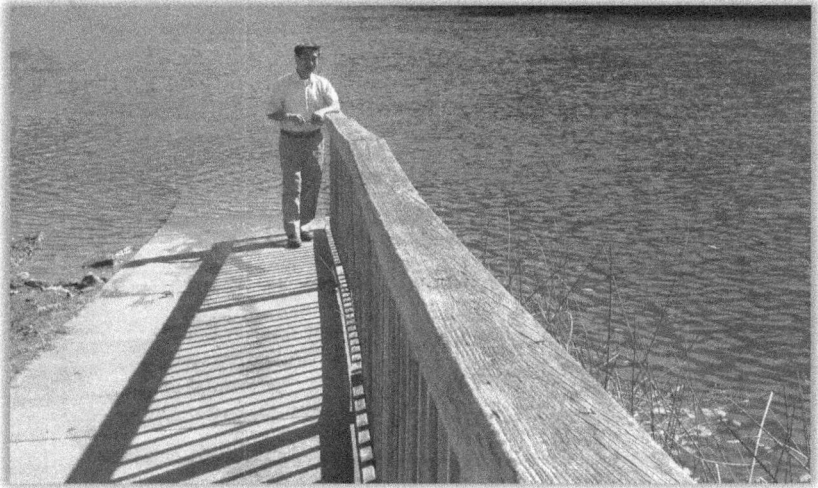

Z3-8 Man-Alone-at-Dock-End

3-25 Power Plant

Power plant burns coal
To turn turbines and generators.
You feel the power come out.

3-26 Presidential Rock Faces

Four presidential faces carved in granite.
Provide a glimpse of history.
Four great leaders we had.

3-27 Shopping Mall

Thousands of displays
Entice you to buy and spend.
People gladly pay.

Z3-9 Pipe-End-Above-Water

3-28   Slums

Humans huddle in poor slums
Forced by circumstances.
We must improve our slums.

3-29   Sydney Opera House

Large petals face the sea,
A beautiful place for spectacular events.
Breathtaking grandeur.

3-30   Washington, DC Mall

Space in the middle of history
Too many places to visit,
Will take many days to tour.

Z3-10 Two-Boys-Swimming

Section 4
Plants and Flowers (Flora)

4-00 Flora

They keep on living
Without purpose or reason
They give us beauty.

TABLE OF CONTENTS – SECTION 4

4-01　Azaleas

Buds fill the stems.
Azalea flowers aglow
With whites, pink, and red.

4-02　Bamboos

Winds ripple the tops
Of resilient bamboo stems.
They bend and survive.

4-03　Bamboo Shoots

Sharp cones rise from the ground
Among the tall bamboo stems.
Life begins for the culms.

Z4-1 Azalea-Flower

4-04 Banana Blossom

The blossom comes out.
It turns into a banana fruit,
Delicious and sweet.

4-05 Betel Nuts

Crimson betel nuts,
Form a bouquet on the crown.
There's beauty in numbers.

4-06 Bitter Melons

Bitter melons on vines
Hang like huge jade gems.
Cook as a fancy dish.

Z4-2 Magnolia-Flower

4-07 Camanchile

Green camanchile pods turn red
And burst with white flesh and black seeds.
Beauty with a unique taste.

4-08 Cashew

A cashew fruit is unusual,
Its seed hangs exposed, outside,
Not inside the fruit.

4-09 Cattails

Reeds with hotdog tops,
Gently sway with the wind,
Grow on the wet marsh.

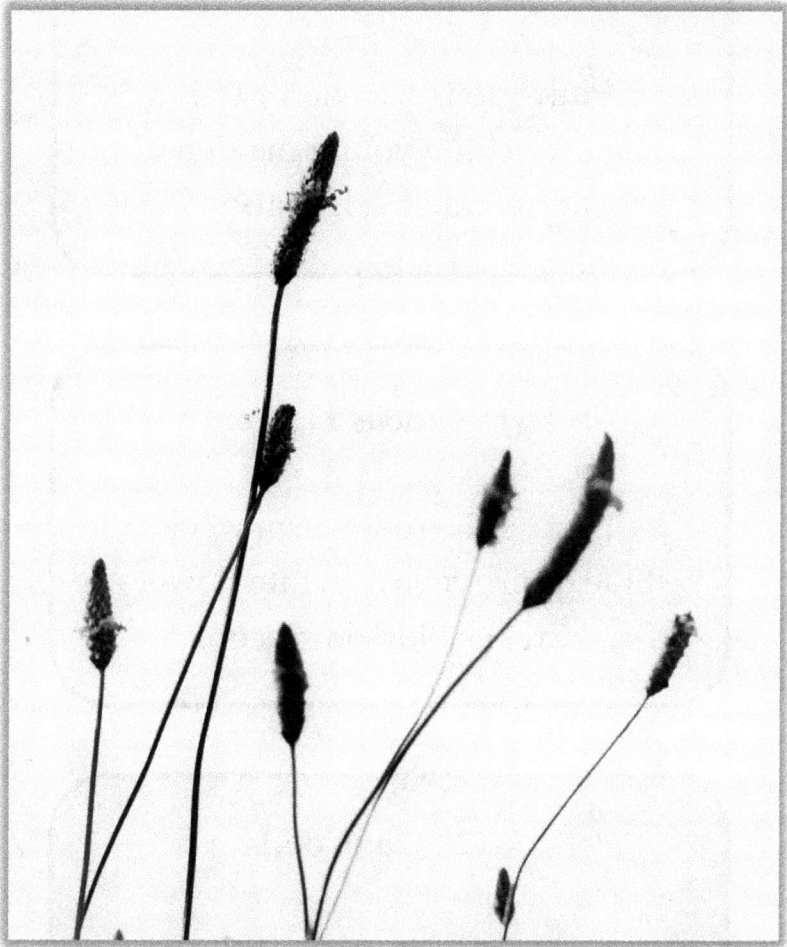

Z4-3 Weed-Flowers

4-10   Cherry Buds

Pink buds on a cherry tree
Like blushing young maidens,
They exude fresh beauty.

4-11   Crocus Flowers

During the first warm week
Blue, pink, yellow, white flowers
Crocus blossoms peep.

4-12   Dogwoods

Dainty crossed petals
Pink or white with a yellow center,
Dogwood flowers bless you.

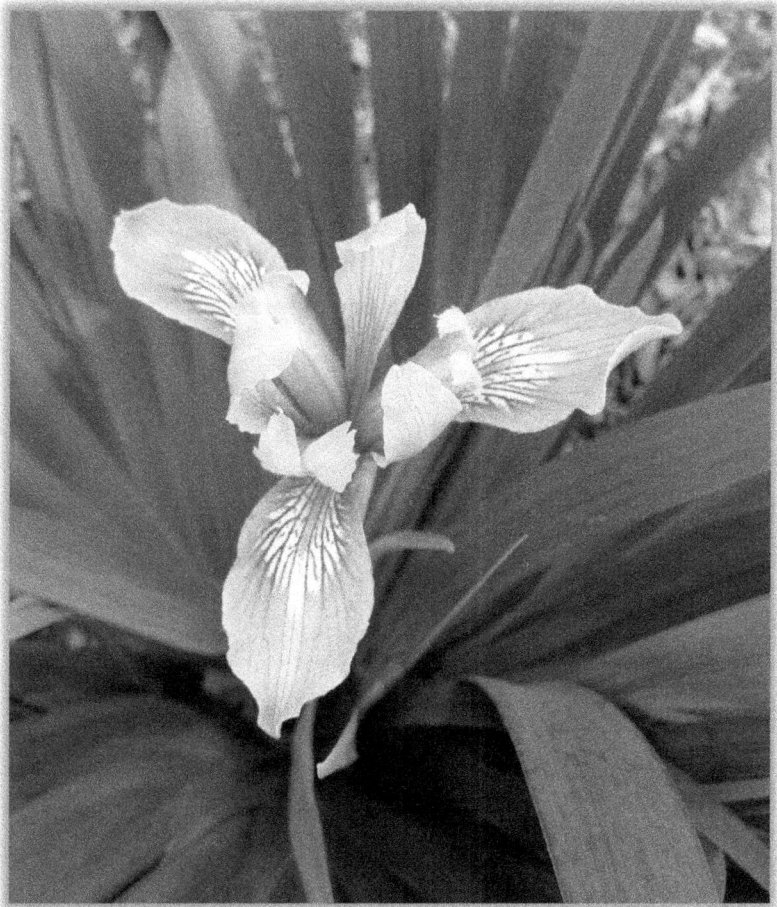

Z4-4 Iris-Flower

4-13 Durian

Durian is smelly,
But tastes sweeter than honey.
It is the forbidden fruit.

4-14 Eggplants Purple

Fruit with purple shades
Rows of eggplants bear plenty.
They make unique dishes.

4-15 Ficus

Dark green shiny leaves
With menacing roots from the trunk.
It is a competitive tree.

Z4-5 Ivy-on-Wall

4-16   Flowers

Fragrance and colors galore
Last for a brief period,
Nature's beauty crown.

4-17   Fruits

Greens, yellows, reds, and browns
Ensconce seeds for the future.
Nature's bounty harvest.

4-18   Heliconia

Pendulous blossoms
Heliconias hang like earrings
Red bracts stand out.

Z4-6 Heliconia-Flower

4-19 Hibiscus

Hibiscus pink and yellow
Show crown of colors on green stems
Their nectars attract bees.

4-20 Jackfruit

Spiney and large jackfruits
Hang on trunks and stems
Full of sweet delights.

4-21 Lanzones

Like brown ochre grapes,
Lanzones tastes infinitely better.
You want to eat more.

Z4-7 Hibiscus-Flower

4-22 Macopa

Pink and white macopa fruits
Hang with bell-shaped blushing colors.
They are sweet and tart.

4-23 Mahogany Tree Rows

Tree trunks lined straight,
Green mahogany leaves form the crown,
Ready for sunshine.

4-24 Maple Leaves

Reddish maple leaves
Among the yellow-green leaves
Announce autumn's start.

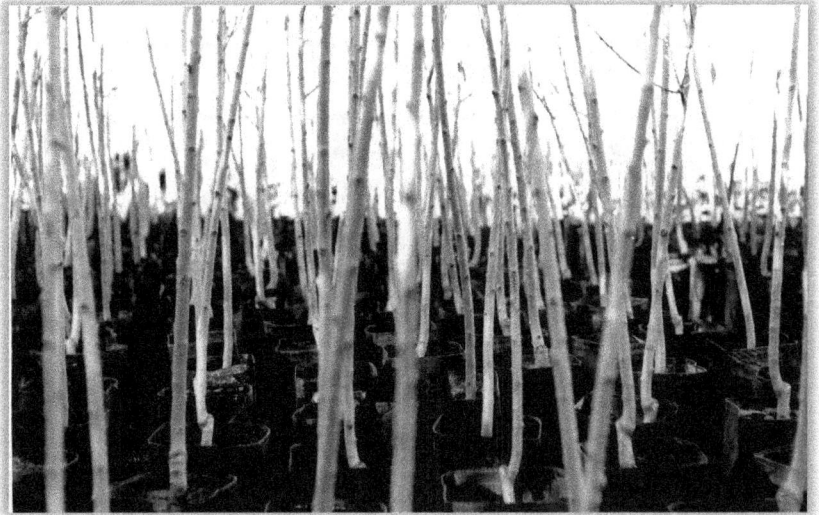

Z4-8 Tree-Seedlings

4-25 Pansies

Colored blooms surround
Light green thin stems and leaves.
Their beauty is delicate.

4-26 Papaya

Ripe papaya fruit
Shows hint of yellow on green
Has the taste of paradise.

4-27 Peonies

Peonies in full bloom
Open and bask in the warm sun
Pink like luscious lips.

Z4-9 Papaya-Fruit

4-28   Plants

Plants are living creations,
Immobile, yet they go on and on.
They adapted for longevity.

4-29   Redbud Clusters

Pink redbuds on grey branches,
Clusters delight the eyes,
Mark spring's arrival.

4-30   Redbud Tree

Redbuds explode in pink,
The laden tree looks unreal.
Nature displays its blush.

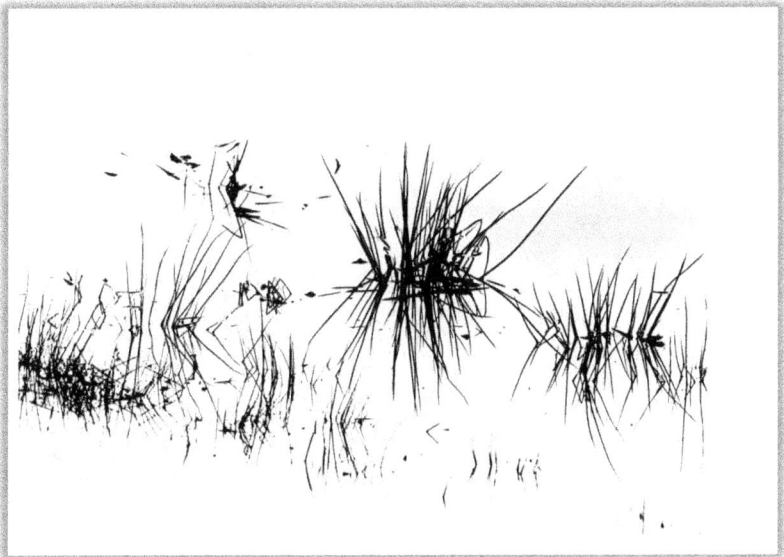

Z4-10 Grass-on-Riverbank

4-31 Squash Flowers

Morning yellow flowers
Beckoning amongst the vines,
Waiting for insects.

4-32 Saguaro

Prickly trees stand still,
Brown trunks filled with water.
Life thrives in the desert.

4-33 Summer Okra

Yellow flowers turn green
Stems hold pointed fruit,
Great fried or steamed.

Z4-11 Cut-Tree-Trunks-Detail

4-34 Tomatoes

Green tomatoes turn yellow,
Then red, waiting to be picked.
Glistening, sweet, and delicious.

4-35 Vine on Trunk

A vine clings to a tree trunk.
Vines aim to climb high,
To rise above the bushes.

4-36 Wild Wheat

Furry-tailed wild wheat
Grows around the summer meadow,
Decorates the land.

Z4-12 Vine-on-Wall

Section 5
Animals and Creatures (Fauna)

5-00 Fauna

Life makes more life.
Creatures move and feel.
Inorganic matter cannot do these.

TABLE OF CONTENTS – SECTION 5

TITLE   PAGE

5-01   Bee on Thistle

It is a winsome sight
Of a black bee on a pink thistle
Gathering sweet nectar.

5-02   Birds

Birds are awesome creatures
That dance in the air, above the earth.
We should enjoy nature's show.

5-03   Carabao

A carabao is a working beast
To till and cultivate the land.
It pulls plows and sleds.

Z5-1 *Three-Carabaos*

5-04   Cicadas

Cicadas wait in silence
For the evening stillness,
Then they sing loud and long.

5-05   Crickets

Crickets singing non-stop
On swaying willow trees
Evoke summer night memories.

5-06   Crows

Black crows caw and play.
They are like black dots that move
Between bare branches.

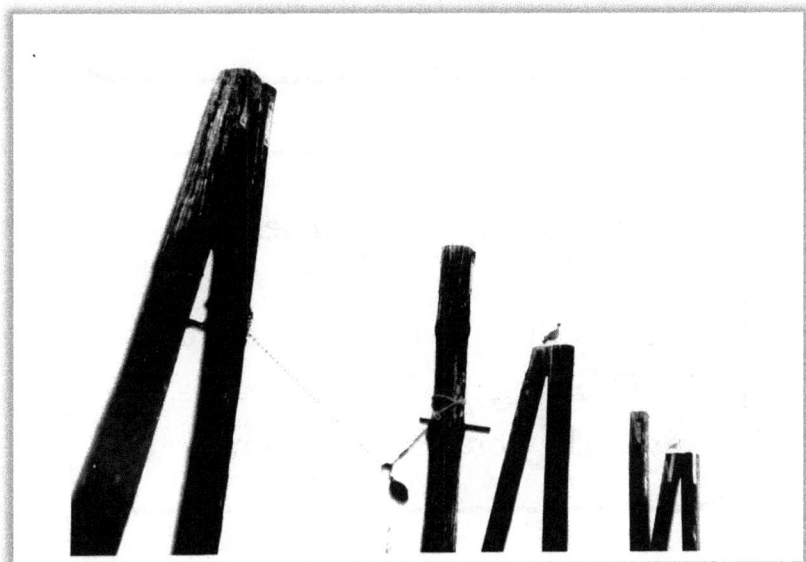

Z5-2 Bird-Atop-Pole

5-07 Donkeys

Donkeys are docile and strong
They are ugly, smell bad, but useful
They are hard workers.

5-08 Dragonflies

Dragonflies hover above the reeds
Deciding to touch the leaves.
They breed by the pond.

5-09 Dragons

Friendly or malevolent,
Dragons are beasts fancied by kids
As if they are real.

Z5-3 Snail-on-Pavement

5-10   Elephants

A herd of elephants
Trek to the waterhole, babies and all.
They show strong family bonds.

5-11   Fish Jumps

Fish jumps arcing above the lake
Ripples spread on water's surface,
Splash sound, then calm returns.

5-12   Horses

Horses are elegant and strong.
They are bred for running.
Power and beauty combined.

Z5-4 Water-Fountain-Sprays

5-13 Jellyfish

Transparent jellyfish
Tentacles shine, move and dance
Always in slow motion.

5-14 Leopards

Leopards have spots
Dotting their sleek bodies.
A rare sight on the plains.

5-15 Lion

A lion moves with stealth
As it focuses on its prey.
Power makes the catch.

Z5-5 Playground-Swings

5-16 Longhorns

Longhorns on big bodies
Roam the wide Southeast grasslands
Hooves move constantly.

5-17 Marlin

Marlin flying fish
Displays jump as a silver flash.
Fights and trashes when hooked.

5-18 Meerkats

Meerkats looking out,
Scouting predators or prey.
They feast on scorpions.

Z5-6 Shadows-Light-and-Man

5-19   Monarch Butterflies

When monarchs migrate,
Their delicate wings propel them
For thousands of miles.

5-20   Mustangs

Wild horses roaming
Freely in Texas plains
Embody Freedom

5-21   Nest

Twigs and grass make nests
Lodged among the branches.
First they hold eggs, then birdies.

Z5-7 Parking-Lot-4Levels

5-22 Parrots

Multi-colored parrots
Display nature's best hues.
Watch them but don't shoot.

5-23 Rabbits

Rabbits hop and run,
White tails and long ears bounce,
Then stop, stare at you.

5-24 Salmon Migrating

They want to return
To the place where they were born,
To lay their eggs, then die.

Z5-8 Lights-and-Bench

5-25 School of Fish

Thousands form one body,
Creating new shapes fluidly.
It is their defense.

5-26 Seashells

Seashells washed ashore
By the surf and lapping waves
Once held life in the sea.

5-27 Sharks

Sharks reign supreme
Among the water creatures.
They are dangerous.

Z5-9 Water-Fountain-Detail

5-28 Snails

Snails are slow.
Would you not be slow too
If you carried your home?

5-29 Snakes

Snakes are vile temptresses,
Have nature's worst reputation.
They just slither.

5-30 Squirrels

Bright-eyed and furry,
They expertly move between branches.
Their jumps are blurs.

Z5-10 Happy-Girl-with-Heavy-Load

5-31 Starlings

Hundreds of black starlings
Tweet as they make mobile art
Move fluidly as one.

5-32 Swans

Swans float in silence.
Curved necks adorn the surface lake
Make graceful ballet moves.

5-33 Termites

Termites dwell under
But can build huge earth mounds.
They are earth architects.

Z5-11 Birds-Above-Hillside

5-34 Trouts

Active tricky trouts
Are the best game against anglers.
Fishing is relaxing.

5-35 Turtles

S-l-o-w and plodding,
They evolved over millennia.
Turtles show patience.

5-36 Wolf Pack

A wolf pack has focus
Members work together to hunt.
Coordinated moves catch prey.

Z5-12 Birds-Atop-Concrete-Wall

Section 6
The Earth

6-00 Our Planet

Round, fragile, and life-giving,
It holds the land, sea, water, air, and us.
It is our only home.

TABLE OF CONTENTS – SECTION 6

6-01   Air

Air envelopes the earth
Still or moving, it affects all,
Synonymous with life.

6-02   Aurora Borealis

They are glowing displays
Of electrons and photons,
Nature's light show.

6-03   Brooks and Rills

Winding brooks and rills
Depict life's meandering turns.
Let us listen to their murmurs.

Z6-1 Farm-Plant-Rows

6-04   Carbon

Carbon is a miracle element
Comes in different forms
Synonymous with plants.

6-05   Clouds

Wisps of dark and white
Flowing, moving, appearing on and off,
Clouds may condense to rain.

6-06   Cornfields

They grow in vast fields
On the flat Midwest plains.
Cornfields yield food.

Z6-2 Buri-Palm-Trees

6-07 Dark Space

Space appears dark and infinite
When no light reaches our eyes.
It is mainly empty.

6-08 Deluge

Too much rain and water
Makes wet and muddy fields.
Deluge is dangerous.

6-09 Desert Dunes

Dry sandhills undulate.
The vista is foreboding
To unprepared travelers.

Z6-3 Concrete-Walkway-on-Water

6-10 Deserts

Deserts seem desolate.
Yet they teem with life and drama
Of desert flora and fauna.

6-11 Double Rainbow

Nature surprises us
With two rainbows together
Doubling the awesome view.

6-12 Drought

Parched land, wilting plants
Are waiting, hoping for rain.
They adjust and endure.

Z6-4 Eaves-Building-Corner

6-13 Earthquakes

Earthquakes reset the balance
Of mighty forces on the earth's surface.
They create stability.

6-14 Evening Light

The evening light of the setting sun
Paints the far horizon with yellow.
Marks the end of another day.

6-15 Eye of the Hurricane

The eye of the hurricane is still.
Walls of air and water swirling around
Wreak havoc below.

Z6-5 Bush-Against-Wall

6-16   Fire

Fire starts as a slow burn
Then leaps, crackles, and sizzles.
Controlled, it is safe and useful.

6-17   Forest Fires

The hills erupt red with flames.
Fire consumes all in its path
Leaving black when done.

6-18   Hurricane

Hurricanes are air united
To make spiraling behemoths.
That cause havoc below.

Z6-6 Stone-Wall-with-Shadow

6-19 Iceberg

An iceberg is solid water afloat.
The tip belies the huge mass below.
It is treacherous.

6-20 Icy Road

Patches of black ice
Cover the lonesome winding road
Trap the careless driver.

6-21 Lakes

They have water surrounded by land
Seas are wide, rivers are narrow
But lakes are in between.

Z6-7 Tires-on-Rack

6-22   Oxygen

Oxygen is life,
Life evolved to use it.
It enabled life on earth.

6-23   Plains

Flat plains go for miles.
Farm homes are very far apart.
Fill the wide expanses.

6-24   Planet Earth

Earth is our only home
Now and in the future.
Take care of it. Now!

Z6-8 Flag-USA

6-25 Plateau

Plateaus are hard to climb.
They flatten at the top.
Where they look like the plains.

6-26 Raging Mud Slides

Rains pour upon hills
Create slurries that race down.
Mud shows its power.

6-27 Rain and Sunshine

Rain and sunshine
One defines the other
We need them both.

Z6-9 Dogwood-Flower

6-28 Rivers

Murmuring rivers
Flow, gurgle, and meander.
Water avoids obstacles.

6-29 Rocks

Rock outcroppings wait
Silently along the hillside
For millennia to come and go.

6-30 Snowfall

Soft silent snowfalls
Blanket the dreary landscape
Etched bare trees on white.

Z6-10 Building-Columns-Detail

6-31   Soil

Soil nurtures plant life,
Provides anchor for growth.
Do not call it dirt.

6-32   Special Clouds

Iridescent clouds
Drape the blue sky canvas
Like rainbow pieces.

6-33   Storm

Winds swirl, form dark clouds
Then, lightning flashes and thunder roars.
The storm has arrived.

Z6-11 Construction-Demolition

6-34 Tornado

A tornado is a vertical evil,
That spins and destroys at the center.
Silent, but sucks with a roar.

6-35 Tsunami

Tsunami waves
Are caused by ocean landmass shifts.
They are quick destroyers.

6-36 Valleys

Two mountains peaks form a valley.
Water flows at the bottom,
Where civilizations thrive.

Z6-12 Biker-in-Tunnel

6-37   Vast Oceans

Water, water everywhere.
Surface forever undulating.
Oceans engulf the earth.

6-38   Volcanoes

A volcano is contained angst.
After years of quiet unease,
The mountain has a tantrum.

6-39   Water

Water is life's juice
Unappreciated until it is not there
It is life's essence.

Z6-13 Boy-in-Pipe

6-40 Water Flows Around Stone

Water rushing down
Finds stone and flows around it.
So should we conduct our lives.

6-41 Waves

Salty water foams.
Their undulations are mesmerizing.
Rising and ebbing constantly.

6-42 Wind blowing

Wind blowing and swirling
Blow fallen leaves on the ground
Tree tops sway like waves.

Z6-14 Bamboo-Culms

Section 7
Moon & Sky

7-00 Moon and Sky

The moon is for everyone.
Its phases affect our moods.
The moon is the queen of the sky.

TABLE OF CONTENTS – SECTION 7

TITLE   PAGE

7-01   Asteroids

Asteroids keep moving.
Gravity affects their trajectory.
They can cause damage if they crash.

7-02   Black Holes

No light ever comes out
They can ingest stars and galaxies.
What's inside is a puzzle.

7-03   Blue Sky

That blue dome above us
Looks empty so we can watch the universe.
Blue photons reach our eyes.

Z7-1 Fireworks-Detail

7-04 Constellations

Hydra and Orion
Are two of many constellations we can see.
They are far and mysterious.

7-05 Dark Matter

Dark matter is the unseen mass.
It accounts for the extra gravity pull.
It remains strange for now.

7-06 Eternity

Has the universe always existed?
Do you believe in eternity?
Yes, if you accept infinity.

Z7-2 Construction-Reinforcing-Bars

7-07   Far Stars and Galaxies

All are mirrors to know our own.
We watch their birth, life, and death
So we will know ours.

7-08   Force and Mystery

Forces operate
The workings of the universe.
We know and feel them.

7-09   Galaxies

Galaxies are big groups
Of billions of stars around black holes.
They look small because they are far.

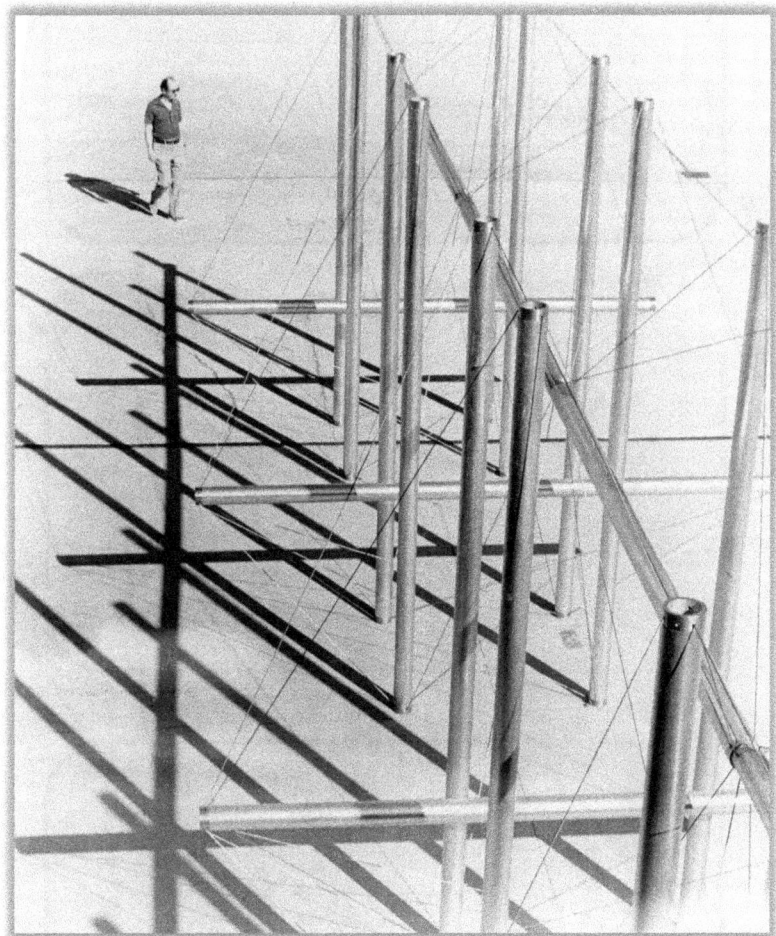

Z7-3 Construction-Stainless-Steel-Art

7-10   Gravity

Gravity is universal,
Makes masses attract one another.
Invisible, yet effective.

7-11   Halo Moon

A halo around the moon
Foretells of rain very soon,
It is time to sow seeds.

7-12   Hubble Telescope

Hubble is a space telescope.
It encircles the earth and sends back images
With amazing reach and clarity.

Z7-4 Windmills

7-13 International Space Station

ISS is a habitat in space
Where astronauts visit and learn
About living in space.

7-14 Jupiter

Jupiter is gigantic and dense.
It is bright; with a strong gravity.
It deflects objects from reaching Earth.

7-15 Mars Landscapes

Mars has barren landscapes,
Untouched since the planet was born.
Mars is near but alien to us.

Z7-5 Stacked-Pallets

7-16 Meteors

Shooting star streaks
Among the twinkling sky dots
They flare out then vanish.

7-17 Milky Way

The Milky Way is our galaxy.
Other stars may also harbor life.
Our sun is just one of many.

7-18 North Star, Polaris

The brightest star in the Small Dipper
Appears stationary night after night,
And has guided ancient seafarers.

Z7-6 Utility-Pipes

7-19 Permanence

Permanence is temporary.
Changes go on forever.
Do not ignore this.

7-20 Pluto

Pluto is small, far and dark,
But it is full of active geology.
It deserves to be a planet.

7-21 Saturn

A unique planet with rings
Of ice and rock pieces
A jewel circling the sun.

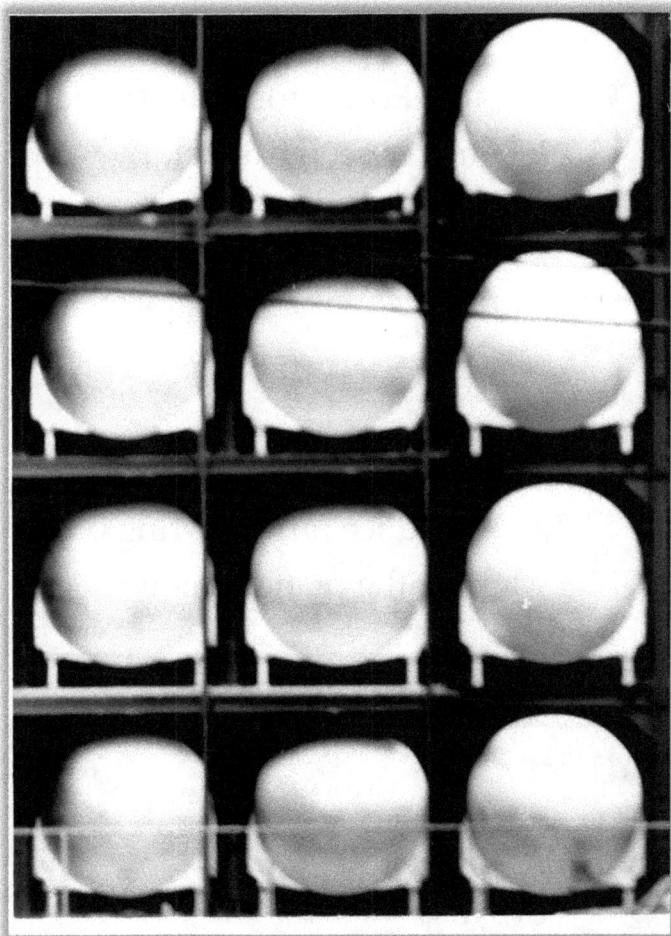

Z7-7 Steam-Tanks

7-22   Saturn Hexagons

Saturn hexagons are huge,
Clouds and storms form the shape.
Geometry seen from afar.

7-23   Saturn Rings

Saturn rings are beautiful.
Rocks and ice form the rings,
Making the planet unique.

7-24   Solar Eclipse

The moon covers the sun briefly,
So, it gets dark during daytime,
Causing anxiety.

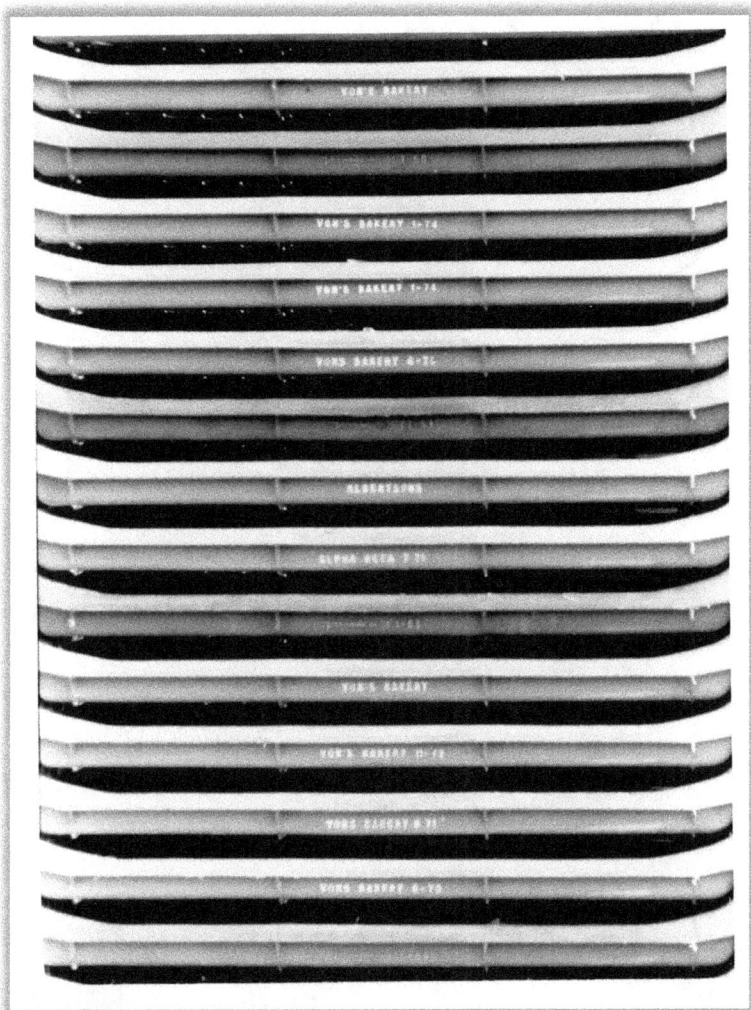

Z7-8 Stacked-Trays

7-25   Space

Anything away from the earth's surface
We call it space or sky
It appears limitless.

7-26   Space Satellites

Like large insects in space
They appear stationary to the earth
The signals bounce quickly.

7-27   Spiral Galaxies

The Milky Way is a spiral.
It is a common galaxy shape.
Stars swirl around the center.

Z7-9 Power-Electric-Transmission

Section 8
Feelings & Reflections

8-00 Feelings and Existence

In the universe,
We exist, think, feel, and reflect.
We know we are here.

TABLE OF CONTENTS- SECTION 8

TITLE   PAGE

8-01   Anxiety

Anxiety is a feeling
That something bad might happen
You don't know what or when.

8-02   Beauty and Ugliness

Life is beautiful
Ugly appears sometimes.
Beauty comes in many forms.

8-03   Day's End

Tiredness and aching muscles
Are felt at the end of a long day.
The evening pause gives rest.

Z8-1 Peony-Flower-Detail

8-04   Determined

It cannot be done?
Sometimes, it is best not to know.
The impossible cannot be done.

8-05   Dying

Life springs at conception.
Body parts form a living piece.
Dying disconnects all the pieces.

8-06   Faith

Faith transcends logic.
You feel a need for something
That is the ultimate remedy.

Z8-2 Hands-Old-Woman

8-07   Fate and Chance

Fate: we will soon know
Chance: we expect but don't know
The rest: we don't know.

8-08   Fear

Fear is a belief
That something bad might happen
Conquer it and move on.

8-09   Future

The future is after the now.
A myriad of things can happen
Between now and then.

Z8-3 Boy-and-Safety-Tubes

8-10 God and Us

We pretend to know
There is one who cares about us.
God provides comfort and answers.

8-11 Good and Evil

Good and evil co-exist
With one gone, the other ceases to be.
Just accept this reality.

8-12 Great Mystery of Living

Born helpless, we are always striving.
We are unique in the universe,
Always hoping and reaching.

Z8-4 Cactus-Detail

8-13 Happiness

Happiness is a feeling
That good things happen all around.
It unburdens the heart.

8-14 Hate

Hate goes beyond dislike.
It is the opposite of like or love.
It is not a good emotion.

8-15 Health

Feelings of good health
Make us believe we'll go on forever,
Allows us to enjoy life.

Z8-5 Two-Women-and-Loads

8-16 Hope

Hope is expectation
That something good will happen.
Without it, everything dies.

8-17 Illness

Feeling ill and blue
Causes us to stop and rest
Reminds us to pause.

8-18 Joy

Joy makes life bearable,
And removes sadness and suffering.
Joy is a good feeling.

Z8-6 Boy-on-Pipes

8-19 Kindness

Kindness helps with life's travails,
With words of encouragement and support..
Kindness helps everyone.

8-20 Life Started

The right chemicals
Joined, evolved, and reproduced.
Thus, life started.

8-21 Life's Struggles

Life is dealing with problems.
The solutions we provide define us.
Struggles line paths to greatness.

Z8-7 Balloons-Released

8-22   Life to End

Life on earth will end
When the sun explodes,
Erasing all life patterns.

8-23   Living Moderately

Moderation is key
To have a long and happy life.
Extremes will not last.

8-24   Love

Love, faith, and hope,
All are needed in life,
But love holds the pieces together.

Z8-8 Two-Men-and-Shadows

8-25 Making a Difference

We travel together.
Make others happy, lighten their load.
This lightens our own.

8-26 Meeting and Collaboration

A group will meet.
Members plan to work together
To do something each cannot.

8-27 Past, Present, Future Time

Time marches forward.
It is infinite, with no start, no end.
We experience the brief now.

Z8-9 Trees-and-Clouds

8-28 Randomness and Order

Order and disorder fight.
Order fights entropy to survive,
Otherwise, disorder reigns.

8-29 Role in the Universe

It is presumptuous to think we have a role.
Just be, enjoy life, and help others.
Our role is to observe and record.

8-30 Sadness

Why so sad?
Something happened not to your liking.
You prefer it did not.

Z8-10 Artwork-Palo-Alto1

8-31 Security

Insecurity is uncomfortable
Whether it is real or imagined.
Help minimize this feeling.

8-32 Sick

Being sick is to not be well.
Sickness prevents the enjoyment of life.
Avoid getting sick.

8-33 Sleep

To sleep is to rest and stop
It relieves our burdens and worries.
It can rejuvenate us.

Z8-11 Stacked-Concrete-Blocks

8-34 Thinking

We often think
Of goals, wants, problems, and needs.
But we can just think and be pleased.

8-35 Unknown Future

The dark unknown future
Has labyrinths full of wishes
Asked but not granted.

8-36 Unknown Unknowns

There are things we know
But there are things we don't know,
And there are unknown unknowns.

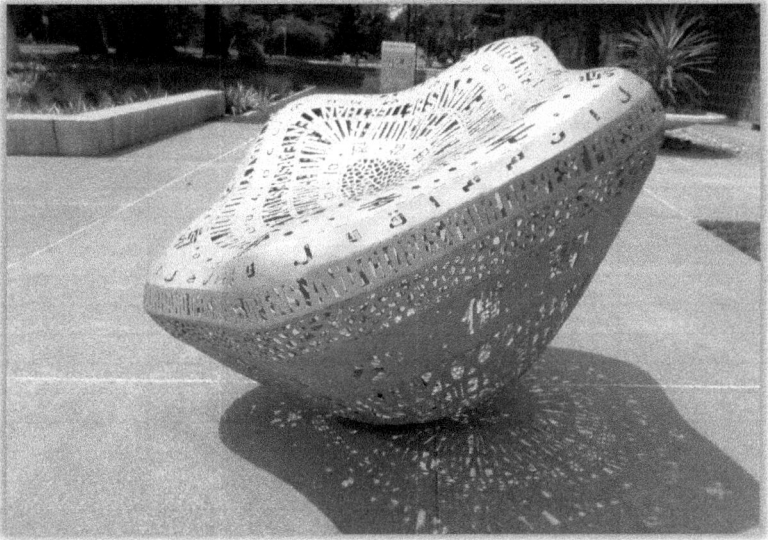

Z8-12 Artwork-Palo-Alto2

INDEX OF HAIKUS

INDEX OF HAIKUS

INDEX OF HAIKUS

INDEX OF HAIKUS

INDEX OF HAIKUS

INDEX OF HAIKUS

INDEX OF ZEN IMAGES

INDEX OF ZEN IMAGES

Author's Note

Orlino C. Baldonado is a retired engineer and is the author of over 30 children's books and over 10 other books. The stories and their settings were inspired by the village in the Philippines where he grew up. He is assisted by or collaborates with his wife Estrella in his writing projects.

Orlino lives in Knoxville, Tennessee. He has two children, Omar and Erika and five grandchildren: Evan, Mia, Noah, Charlotte, and Josephine. Their family owns the media publishing company, ecEmedia, Inc. Orlino continues to maintain his involvement with and make frequent trips to his former hometown, Santa Maria, Ilocos Sur, Philippines.

Illustrators' Note

Rosanna R. Dalilis is the production coordinator of ecEmedia, Inc. Rosanna is always interested in learning new things. She is thankful to ecEmedia for allowing her to experience lay-outing and photo editing projects.

Melvin S. Dato is working as an internet administrator in a state college. Additional interests include graphic designs, digital drawings and digital publishing. His wife, Juyren Dee U. Dato and daughter, Nevaeh Rhaine U. Dato are his inspirations in all his accomplishments.

Rosanna and Melvin are both from Suso, Santa Maria, Ilocos Sur, Philippines. Haiku and Zen is one of their many projects published by ecEmedia.

More Stories from
ec℮media
by Orlino C. and Estrella C. Baldonado

Princess Stories (Series)
Zacana, the Singing Princess
Zebona, the Princess of Birds
Carlotta, the Librarian Princess
Sunyata, the Sunflower Princess
Anzita, the Princess Who Would Not Grow
Jerika, the Sea Princess
Hannah, the Helpful Princess

Extended Aesop Stories (Series)
The Greedy Dog
The Ant and the Grasshopper
The Tortoise and the Hare
The Boy Who Cried Wolf
The Two Roosters
The Fox Who Lost His Tail
The Lion and The Mouse

Enhanced Classic Rhymes (Series)
Itsy Bitsy Spider Extended
Jack & Jill After the Tumble
Humpty Dumpty Revived
Old Ambrocio Had a Farm
Five Little Monkeys Swinging on a Tree

Environmental Series
Mother Penguin and Her Chick
The Two Dolphins
Ofrio, The Sea Otter

Moments ALONE

Yassy, the Sister Pig and the Wolf (Series)
Yassy, the Sister Pig (Background Story)
Yassy Frightens the Wolf
Yassy Pummels the Wolf
Yassy Prepares Bad Bread for the Wolf
Yassy Irritates the Wolf
Yassy Taunts the Wolf

Buyog and Trella: A Bee and Butterfly Story
Mally & Draky, Loyal Pair of Mallards
Trees & Blooms-The Legacy of Rene and Nena Lapido

Buy them (as e-book or paperback) from **www.amazon.com**.
Check the Publishers Website: **www.ecEmedia.net.**
Contact the authors via email: **orlinob@gmail.com**